the backyard kids ™

Regina Oakes & Danielle Devine

Dedication

To our children, this one's for you.
To our husbands, this would have been impossible without you.
To snow days, hot chocolate, and endless childhood memories.

Text Copyright 2023 by Backyard Publications, LLC

For information regarding permission,

author visits, or inquiries please email: backyardkids215@gmail.com

© Backyard Publications, LLC

ISBN # 9798858531128

Don't turn the page! See that sticker?!
It says TOP SECRET!

TOP SECRET

Journal Guide of Contents

DO NOT OPEN THIS JOURNAL

(I MEAN IT)

I seriously mean it!!
Do not turn to the next page!

Somerville Charter School Yearbook Photos

Jayden Bell
"I know the words to
any song... Test me"

Sunny Sanchez
"Debate team to news
anchor - just wait."

Kolten Ryan
"Is it baseball season
yet?!"

Duke Ortiz
"BAY ROAD CREW"

BASH BROS
"Two for the price of
one here."

Jack James
"You can never have too
many basketball jerseys"

Amir Youseff
"I'm hungry, you
hungry too?"

Harper Nguyen
"Keep the Earth
clean"

Ellie Bell

~~Nora Smith~~
"First female president right
here"

Well, you turned the page I see. Since you are a daredevil like us, you'll fit right in. Let me tell you about a story. It's not every day you find a journal written by a bunch of kids, right?

WRONG.

Here in Somerville, it's totally normal to write in journals. It all started with Coach Rod's epic baseball team. The story is simple:

- Baseball team STINKS
- Coach bans technology
- Kids create a journal to pass around the team
- Baseball team went from the WORST to the BEST...

Wait wait wait...

I'm not going to spoil it. That's a story for a different day. But I do have another story to tell you. Sit back, relax, and grab a cup of hot chocolate. We are going for a snowy ride.

ENTRY ONE

Sunday, January 2
Back to school, UGH

Name: Duke Ortiz
Birthday: April 28
Favorite things: cereal,
sports highlights, weekends

You'll be reading my entries
here until I pass the journal
on!

Glorious, magical, winter break was coming to an
end... Sadly, it was the night before the dreaded
return to school. I think adults call it

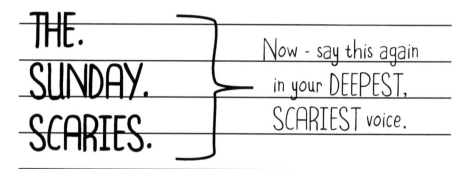

THE.
SUNDAY.
SCARIES.

Now - say this again
in your DEEPEST,
SCARIEST voice.

To make matters worse, grouchy, old Principal Pringlesnap
scheduled a 102-question math test for tomorrow - the
day we return to the dreaded prison!!! How diabolical,
how rude, how evil!!

Rumor has it Pringlesnap has worked at Somerville
Charter School for over 200 years. **Be warned** what
you're about to see on the next page may trigger
nightmares.

ANATOMY OF A ~~MONSTER~~ PRINCIPAL

PENCIL: to hand out detention slips. ALWAYS attached to her

HORNS: to poke students late for class (OR NO REASON AT ALL)

TEETH: to shred hall passes written by teachers

TAIL: to whip students behind her if caught laughing

ID BADGE: to access her dungeon

CLAWS: to help with traction when chasing students

MOLE: we don't know about this one, but here is a close-up view. We call it BIG BERTHA

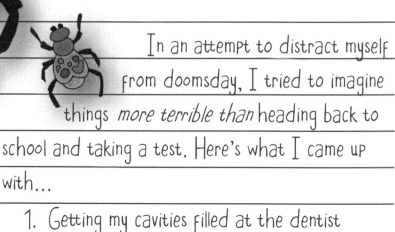

In an attempt to distract myself from doomsday, I tried to imagine things *more terrible than* heading back to school and taking a test. Here's what I came up with...

1. Getting my cavities filled at the dentist
2. Bugs taking over the world
3. Losing the championship game

My brainstorming was interrupted by a LOUD sound coming from the TV. I darted to the living room to see what was happening! My mom turned to me and shouted, "Honey-bunny ...come quick - you have to hear what they're saying on the news!!"

Also, don't tell anyone she calls me hunny bunny, ok?!? It would ruin my reputation!

14

BREAKING  WEATHER REPORT

flashed across the

screen!!! We listened as the news reporter said,

"Biggest snowstorm to hit the northeast part of the

country, hitting hardest in the City of Somerville."

Was this real? Winter break may not end after all?!

Let me break it down with the only equation you will see

in this journal (I hope).

SOMERVILLE STREETS
+   SNOW
―――――――――――――――
= NO BUSES
= NO KIDS
= SCHOOL CLOSED
= EXTENDED BREAK

We couldn't leave this to chance, so my mom and me got to work!

COMMENCE
'Operation Snow Dance'

What is 'Operation Snow Dance'?

A magical and hilarious set of activities done by kids (and cool parents!!) around the world to make snow fall from the sky! It has worked so well in past winters that it has a scientifically proven 90 percent success rate.

'Operation Snow Dance' Activated

My mom and I did every snow dance activity ever used. NOT ONCE. NOT TWICE. BUT THREE TIMES. We ran around the house like kids in a candy shop. It was epic.

During 'Operation Snow Dance' Mom and I:

- Turned our pajama pants inside out
- Put a spoon in the freezer
- Set a white crayon on the windowsill
- Grabbed a bag of marshmallows from the pantry, THEN flushed them down the toilet (this one was so fun, she made me promise not to tell dad)
- Shouted "SNOW DAY" into the freezer
- Ate ice cream straight from the container
- Played oldies on the radio and danced around the kitchen table
- Fetched the spoon from the freezer and placed it under my pillow before the night's sleep!

SIDENOTE: Mom tells me she lived through an epic snowstorm when she was a kid. THIS is exactly what she did to make it happen. Fingers crossed it works again this time!

Principal Pringlesnap, on the other hand, wouldn't call for a snow day even if elephants were falling from the sky. Here at Somerville Charter School, kids say she has a secret door behind the bookcase in her ~~dungeon~~ office that leads to her bed. Meaning

SHE.
NEVER.
LEAVES.
SCHOOL.

So, kids - this has been a thrilling run, but Operation Snow Dance was basically for nothing. It's silly to think Pringlesnap would actually cancel school.

Exhausted from the snow dance activities with Mom, I got ready for bed. Just before I closed my eyes, I looked out the window and saw a shooting star.

I closed my eyes and I wished like I have **NEVER** wished before.

Can you guess what I wished for?

ENTRY TWO

Monday, January 3
Will there be snow?

Alright - it's still me, Duke, writing. I promise you'll meet the rest of the crew soon... But I have a lot to tell you.

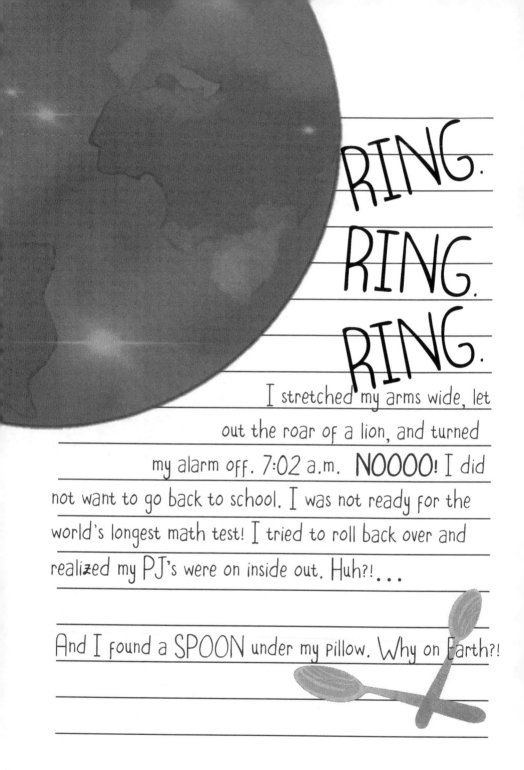

RING.

RING.

RING.

I stretched my arms wide, let out the roar of a lion, and turned my alarm off. 7:02 a.m. **NOOOO!** I did not want to go back to school. I was not ready for the world's longest math test! I tried to roll back over and realized my PJ's were on inside out. Huh?!...

And I found a SPOON under my pillow. Why on Earth?!

WAIT. A. MINUTE.

I bolted from my bed to the window. I made
one final plea to Mother Nature (you know, the
lady in the sky who controls all
things weather-related).

With one **BIG**, deep
breath, I opened the
blinds and was greeted
with a...

Winter Wonderland

I slid down the railing to the living room. NO TIME FOR STAIRS TODAY

I screamed for my mom at the top of my lungs,

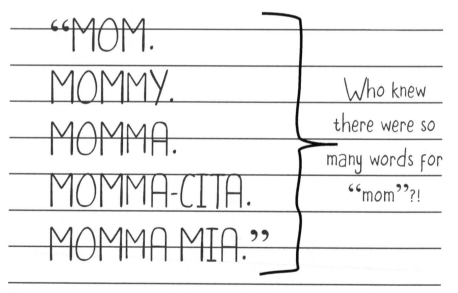

"MOM.
MOMMY.
MOMMA.
MOMMA-CITA.
MOMMA MIA."

Who knew there were so many words for "mom"?!

Finally, there she was. "Mom, is this real life?" Without saying a word - she waved her cellphone in the air.

Somerville Charter School

School is CLOSED for ONE WEEK due to the ongoing blizzard. Stay safe.

SCHOOL IS CLOSED. FOR ONE FULL WEEK.

- SEE YA LATER, PRINCIPAL PRINGLESNAP
- BYE, HORRIBLE-102 QUESTION MATH TEST
- FAREWELL, LEFTOVER SCHOOL LUNCHES
- AND HELLOOOOOOO EXTENDED WINTER BREAK

There was only one order of business that had to be handled during this snow week... DOCUMENT EVERYTHING! That's exactly why I created this journal!

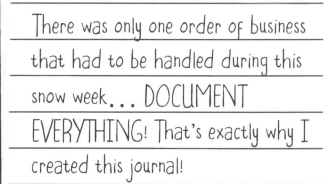

There are already 52 inches of pure white snow on the ground - but it won't be white for long! Just wait until my PUPPY, Hank, does his morning business. WAIT - the snow is taller than him... How the heck will he tinkle outside?! (This sounds like a problem for dad to solve).

> Can you believe that's over 4 feet of snow?!

There may be 52 inches of snow on the ground, BUT I was NOT going to treat this day any different from the rest. So, I showered, got dressed, shoved the journal in my pocket, and went to knock for my best friend, Sunny.

When I opened the door to make my way to her house

I was presented with one teeny, tiny problem....

It's official, we were

SNOWED IN!!! ❄

To get to Sunny's house, I had to...

Shovel.

And shovel.

And guess what?

I SHOVELED SOME MORE.

I shoveled until my knees shook, my teeth chattered...
until icicles started growing from my nose.

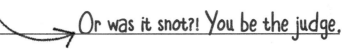 Or was it snot?! You be the judge.

Finally, I could see Sunny's house. I only had a few more
feet left until I was at her front door...

Shovel, scoop, scrape.
Shovel, scoop, scrape.
Shovel, scoop... Cough, cough, cough.

Man, shoveling is no joke - it was serious
exercise!!!

The next time the shovel hit the snow, it felt *VERY, VERY* different. Almost like the shovel forgot how to shovel!!! I tried again - harder this time. With all my might I slammed it into the snow.

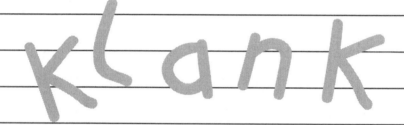

Ok - that was NOT snow. Snow makes sounds like **CRUNCH** and **SCRUNCH** and **CRUMP**. Not klank.

What was it? I began digging with my hands. Did I strike gold? Did I dig all the way to China?

At that moment, Sunny came running from her house, "Duke, Duke, Duke!! Do you believe this? A real-life snow day! Not one, not two, not three days... we are off for SEVEN STRAIGHT DAYS. Just when I thought we were headed back to school!"

But there was no time for chit-chat.

Sunny joined in, we looked like dogs digging in dirt. SNOW. FLYING. EVERYWHERE.

Until we completely unburied IT.

The most mysterious object... EVER.

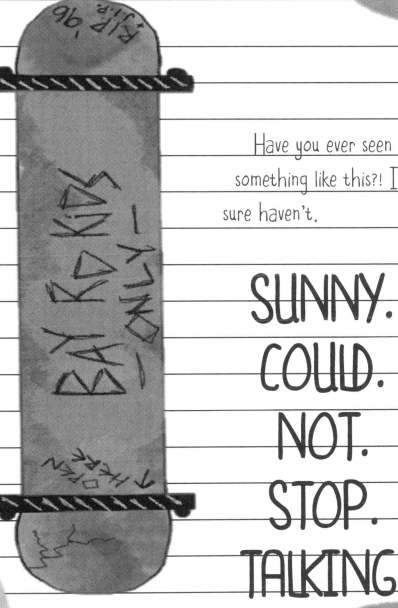

Have you ever seen something like this?! I sure haven't.

SUNNY.
COULD.
NOT.
STOP.
TALKING.

"I've seen something like this on TV – this is a TIME CAPSULE!"

"Who is R.I.P. and J.I.P. ? See the initials in the corner?!"

"How did IT get here?!"

"It says Bay Road kids! That's us! That's our street!"

"Ohhh– it has a lid! Let's open it!"

Things Sunny said

When Sunny gets started, there is no stopping her! Only one thing left to do when she starts spiraling like this.

Sunny- it is your time to shine.

Get it?! I have been saving that joke for a year now... You know, your name is Sunny, like the sun - It shines...

Ok maybe it wasn't as funny as I first thought. But I know you're the only person who can solve this time capsule mystery.

     To the moon,

      Duke

ENTRY THREE

Still Monday, January 3
Time capsule?

Name: Sunny
Love: Reading, ICE CREAAAM
DISLIKES: Duke's farts - EWW! I
am sure you'll see later!!

Sunny Sanchez here. Your journal reporter for all things blizzard related... One day I'm going to be a world-famous reporter on TV! Until then, let's figure out what is going on with this time capsule THINGY-MA-BOB.

Here in Somerville, the Bay Road kids do everything together. So, when me and Duke found the time capsule, we knew we had to open it - but we couldn't do it alone.

That would be breaking the ultimate

GOLDEN RULE

GOLDEN RULE ONE:
If you ever uncover a mysterious item in an epic snowstorm, you must bring all Bay Road kids together.

Ok, so that's not exactly the truth, the whole golden
rule thing... We actually don't have a

GOLDEN RULE!!

What we do have is an unwritten rule...

So, me and Duke got to work, grabbed our shovels, and
made our way around the block. We knocked on
everyone's door and didn't stop until the whole
crew was together.

To appreciate how hard this was to do in 52 inches of snow, I included a detailed map of our street. And let me tell you, it's the best street to grow up on in the City of Somerville.

Somerville ROCKS, Bay Road ROCKS, WE ROCK!

Map of Bay Road

Turn page for number breakdown.

Who's Who Decoder

#1- Kolten's crib: Somerville's baseball pitcher lives here, he is best friends with Jack on the block. Has the biggest collection of baseball cards, EVER!

#2- My house: The place you want to be if you need to know anything Somerville related. Loves dancing and acting in the drama club.

#3- Duke's casa (casa is Spanish for "home") and my ultimate sidekick. He teaches us a new word/phrase every day in Spanish. Today, the phrase was "*hasta luego*" (pretend the *h* isn't there when you say it - it means "see you later")

#4- Harper's palace: Home of all things paint and clay beads. Lover of plants, animals, crystals, and the Earth. We need more people like her.

#5- Jack's house: He would like you to believe that he lives in a mansion! The most business savvy kid out there who despises homework more than ANYONE I know.

#6- Creepy *abandoned* lair: AVOID THIS HOUSE. Ghosts and howling sounds reported here. The worst part, there is an AWESOME tire swing in the backyard- WHAT. A. WASTE.

#7- Nash's house: Known for the 'Toilet Paper Prank of 2022', the 'Fart Gun Palooza of 2023', and so much more. ½ of the BASH BROS (best friends - always together)

#8- Brendan's crib: The other ½ of the BASH BROS lives here, also known for the same WILD mischief as Nash. Come on, you think Nash could pull all that off alone?!

#9- Jayden and Ellie's place: A protective BIG brother and a SPUNKY little sister duo who always make us laugh. Always have each other's back.

#10 Amir's house: Prankster, comedian, epic comic maker. Also known for the takedown of Somerville's rivals, The Philly Blazers!

#3   #2   #1

#4

#10

#5

#9

#6

#7   #8

After the crew was together, we went back to my place and huddled around the time capsule.

"OPEN IT,
OPEN IT,
OPEN IT."

My hands trembled.

A little voice inside my head said, "I wouldn't do it if I were you..." But my hands had a mind of their own and the lid was off before I knew it. I was TERRIFIED to look inside, but the reporter in me HAD to get to the bottom of this story.

... and the bottom of the story was a DEAD END.
Yeah, you read that right. NOTHING WAS
IN THERE. What a cruel joke! All our hard
work to get this THING out from the frozen
ground and it was all one big HOAX!
Hoax is a fancy word for a MEAN
TRICK!

Jack couldn't believe it! He grabbed
the capsule from my hands and shook it.
He jiggled, wiggled, and shook so hard a string fell out
(it was connected to the bottom). He pulled the string,
revealing a trap door...

Jack reached into the secret compartment. Slowly he
pulled out...

TIME CAPSULE ITEMS

R.I.P. & J.I.P. – Blizzard of 1996
11 years old

#1

#2

OPEN:
BAY ROAD KIDS

#3 KBY

#4

#5

#6

Time capsule cataloguer. Read below for a description.
Some items remain a mystery.

#1: A picture of two kids from '96.
It says R.I.P. and J.I.P. under it. This must be a
picture of the kids behind the capsule!

#2: An envelope, ADDRESSED TO US! Do you see that?!?
It says 'OPEN: BAY ROAD KIDS'

#3: Magnetic letters. K, B, Y

#4: WHAT ARE THOSE?! They're weird, but also kind of
cute if you squint your eyes tight. What do they have in their
belly button?!

#5: A plastic ball, that has a little window in it. Words
float in the window and say things like "yes," "no,"
and "ask again later."

#6: A stuffy that is filled with anything but cotton. It's
filled with… BEANS?!?

"Can you believe that one picture in the capsule is from 1996? That is almost 30 years ago?"
- Kolt

"That means the people in the picture must be like 40 years old right now! (they are close to my parents age!) Man, they are really old."
- Jayden

"We need to figure out who these kids were and if they still live here in Somerville!!!"
- Jack

"Kids from the 90s sure had some weird toys."
- Duke

"Ew, who just burped?!"
- Ellie

Convos about the time capsule

Jack quickly interrupted our conversations, waving around the envelope from the capsule. He ripped it open and found a torn letter. He handed the letter to me - and in my best reporter voice...

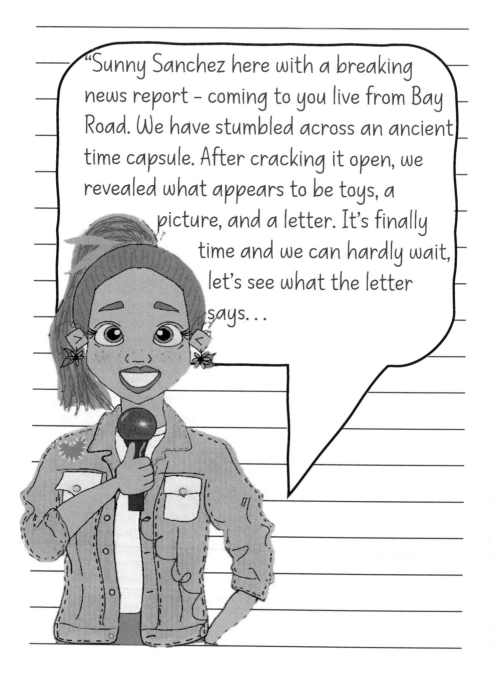

"Sunny Sanchez here with a breaking news report - coming to you live from Bay Road. We have stumbled across an ancient time capsule. After cracking it open, we revealed what appears to be toys, a picture, and a letter. It's finally time and we can hardly wait, let's see what the letter says. . .

Dear Kids Who Found This Time Capsule,

Way to go! Me and my best friend buried this time capsule during the Blizzard of '96. We made it to help pass the time since we lost electricity!

All throughout Somerville we planted clues that will take you on the adventure of a lifetime. **Did we mention there was also an AWESOME reward at the end too?!** Ah, I see we have your attention now!

We hope the clues are still there by the time you come across them! Better hurry up! **Clue #1 is waiting for you on the other side of this note.**

From, RIP and JIP

Time Capsule Clue #1

If you are reading this note of mine,
You've opened a capsule that captures time.

I buried it deep in the dirt of Bay Road,
so future Somerville kids would have a mystery to decode.

Want to find another capsule clue?
Head to Neli's Hill to sled with your crew.

Of course, there's a catch and it is a **must**,
You CANNOT use a sled, **so plan and adjust.**

Once you all sled and have some fun,
Find the tree marked B until the next clue comes undone.

The streetlights suddenly came on, do you know what that means? It's time to get home. I'll send out a note with a plan letting everyone know where to meet.

MEMO: To All Bay Road Kids

We are in for a time capsule scavenger hunt and I seriously want to find the next clue. You want in? Let's do what the clue said...

When? Tomorrow, 10:00 AM
Where? Neli's Hill
What? Sledding, with ANYTHING BUT A SLED! Get creative people!

I wish we could go tonight, but the streetlights ruined that.

Passing the journal to you, Kolt the Bolt.

From the Sun,
Sunny

If you don't know about streetlights, you're lucky. They turn on once it's dark outside and we have to come in when they turn on.

It's about 30 years later and they were 11 at the time... that makes them around 40 now

R.I.P. & J.I.P. - Blizzard of 1996
11 years old

CLUE SUMMARY

- CLUE 1: Neli's Hill. Bring anything but a sled. Look for a tree marked with a B.

Written on time capsule:
R.I.P. + J.I.P '96

These kids must have
lived on Bay Road and
buried the capsule then

ENTRY FOUR

Tuesday, January 4
Sledding with a twist

Name: Kolten Ryan
Birthday: February 6

Lover of all things: baseball, baseball cards, and drawing

Hater of all things: scary, heights, and laundry

I wouldn't be Jack's best friend if I didn't draw attention to the most interesting part of clue #1.

The clue mentioned there was a REWARD at the end of this scavenger hunt.

A REWARD!!!

How can we not talk about it?! I love the idea of finding clues and trying to figure out a mystery, BUT I love the idea of A REWARD even more!!

We made a list of the things we wished the reward would be:

REWARD WISH LIST

1. **Kolten (me):** A signed Babe Ruth baseball card
2. **Bash Bro's:** THE LOUDEST WHOOPIE CUSHION OF ALL TIME
3. **Jayden:** The new pair of Jordan sneakers, limited edition of course
4. **Jack:** A *crisp* $100 bill
5. **Ellie:** A Taylor Swift sweatshirt
6. **Harper:** A new crystal to bring good energy and positive vibes
7. **Duke:** Lifetime supply of tacos
8. **Sunny:** Solve the time capsule mystery

I'd love to see what the Bash Bro's have planned for loudest whoopie cushion, EVER.

Back to business, now! RIP and JIP (the time capsule kids) knew what they were talking about - sledding down a hill with anything *BUT A SLED* was...

Heart-racing,

eye-bulging,

scary,

and WILD!

It was...

STRAIGHT UP SOMERVILLE

Fun!

Time flew like a bird, like a plane, like a loose balloon in the sky. These sleds were SERIOUS excitement!

They may have been too much fun - we couldn't keep control of them! Take a peek on the next page to see what everyone came up with.

ANYTHING but A SLED

Which one is your favorite?!?!

My sled:
wiffle ball bats taped together to make one big sled (did you expect anything else?!?)

Bash Bros:
A double sleeping bag

Ellie:
A baby pool filled with her favorite stuffies

Sunny:
A laundry basket filled with her brothers clothes

Amir:
A flamingo inflatable pool ring

Jayden:
A trash can lid

Jack:
His dad's favorite canoe (he may have gotten grounded for this later)

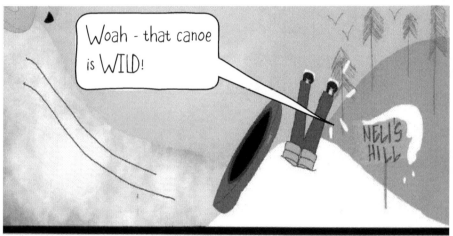

AWESOME

After hours of sledding and making EPIC snow angels, we were FROZEN. We were getting ready to head home when Harper screeched, "STOOOPPP."

Thank goodness she did - we got so caught up in the sledding fun we totally forgot the real purpose of this mission:

Clue #2!!

To make matters worse, we also didn't notice that Ellie was MIA (this means MISSING IN ACTION). Would we ever see her again?

WAIT. You actually kept reading? You must have misunderstood the other page. The last page said:

~~ELLIE.~~ WENT. MISSING.

Ellie - Jayden's little sister!!!!!!!!!

Clue #2 had to wait. We needed to find her, NOW! We yelled at the top of our lungs. We searched high, low, and everywhere in between, but nothing turned up. Which meant only one thing:

IT WAS TIME }

TIME TO TELL OUR MOMS

Dun, dun, dunnnnn

We really didn't want to do this. The Moms would FOR SURE stop our time capsule adventure and ground us for decades! I am talking about serious time here,

Just as we gave up hope, Jayden found snow prints leading into the deep, dark woods. Whew - close call, I'm too young for jail! We still had a big decision to make. Should we go into the deep, dark woods?

A quick game of rock, paper, scissors and our decision was made. We were going to find Ellie...

DEEP DARK WOODS - HERE WE COME!

We tiptoed our way in... the wind howled like a wolf, the trees whistled. As we made our way deeper, we found Ellie's blankie stuck in a bush, blowing in the wind. She had to be close!

Nightfall crept in. Jayden held back tears. He screamed with ALL his might, "ELLLLLLIE!" We heard a soft giggle,

"No sillies, LOOK UP!"

73

ELLIE was stuck - *IN A TREE!* No problem for Jayden, he got her back down to the ground in a flash.

ACTIVATE BIG BROTHER MODE.

"Ellie Marie - wait until I tell Mom... What were you thinking? Have you lost your mind?! Why on Earth would you walk into the woods without ---"

Jayden couldn't finish his sentence. Ellie was grinning from ear to ear and held her hand high in the sky.

It was...the second clue!!!!

Ellie explained, "You were having so much fun. And, and... I didn't want to ruin it by telling everyone we forgot about clue #2. Except me, I totally remembered - 'Once you all sled and have some fun, find the tree marked B until the next clue comes undone' and I found it!!!!"

Man, never underestimate little brothers and sisters. Ellie was clutch. Brave too. She handed me the clue and I read it aloud.

Time Capsule Clue #2

You made it this far, oh what a thrill;
How much fun - sledding down Neli's Hill.

This next clue is a bit more tricky,
But someone will help you figure out this doohickey.

Make your way to the best pizza place in town,
Ask for Doc and remember to 'smile, never frown'.

Jack 'The Snack'-
How cool is this?! We are back at it again, passing journals around. I knew we were onto something when we started our baseball journal last year. But no time for reminiscing, we need to figure this clue out. It isn't much of a mystery in my opinion. The best pizza place in town is Momma Mia's Pizzeria. Hands down.

Their best pie is the upside-down pizza (for those that don't know - cheese on bottom, sauce on top.

PERFECTION. We'll head over there tomorrow as soon as the doors open and ask for this mystery man, "Doc". Fingers crossed we'll find him, I'm kind of nervous, it has been 30 years! What if he doesn't work there anymore?! I need to find this TREASURE and get the REWARD. First thing we have to do is figure out whatever the heck a "doohickey" is... like really - what does this word mean?!

Journal is coming to you Jack.
From, your best bro, Kolt

PS- What are you doing in the winter to keep your side businesses going?! You always have some type of side hustle in hopes to become the first self-made kid billionaire.

What is it? Shoveling snow? Making snowballs and selling them? Hot chocolate stand? SHARE THE DEETS.

R.I.P. & J.I.P. - Blizzard of 1996
11 years old

It's about 30 years later and they were 11 at the time... that makes them around 40 now

Momma Mia's
PIZZERIA

CLUE SUMMARY

- CLUE 1: Neli's Hill. Bring anything but a sled. Look for a tree marked with a B.
- CLUE 2: Go to Momma Mia's Pizzeria, ask for a guy named Doc. Find out what a "doohickey" means.

Written on time capsule:
R.I.P. + J.I.P '96
These kids must have
lived on Bay Road and
buried the capsule then

Please be a crisp, firm $100 bill...

Please be a crisp, firm $100 bill...

Don't mind me, just going to keep wishing for my time capsule reward - maybe it will come true?!

ENTRY FIVE

Wednesday, January 5

Happy Birthday to ME!!

About me:

- Name: Jack James
- They call me Jack 'The Snack'
- I'm an endless pit of hunger, buttered noodles are my FAVORITE
- My birthday is TODAY
- Basketball OBSESSED
- Business owner (see next page)

I always wake up at
the crack of dawn.
Early bird gets the
worm. And let me tell you,
this bird has a business plan -
and a fat, juicy
worm waiting!!

Check out some
of my current
businesses
where I'm the CEO.

A fancy word for
BOSS

Today, when I woke up, I was all business for another reason. I put reminders on everyone's front door. WE HAD NO TIME TO WASTE…

MEMO TO BAY ROAD CREW

DIRECTIONS: Meet at the corner of Bay Road and Stevens Road @ 10:00 AM sharp. Then we'll walk over to Momma Mia's

Ask your parents:

- if they know anyone named "Doc"
- what a "doohickey" is
- if they know anyone with the initials R.I.P. or J.I.P.

Don't make it obvious. Just say you are researching for a school project or something.

I arrived at our meeting spot at 9:30, right on time (according to Dad - a half hour early is on time). I was the first one there, so I started making a snowman, you know, to help pass the time. I must have been in some sort of trance because before I knew it, a snowman was staring back at me and he looked just like....

"COACH ROOODDDDDDDD"

Duke yelled as he walked up with Sunny and the other Bay Roaders.

I couldn't believe my eyes. In all his frozen glory, this snowman was a SPITTING image of Coach Rod. If you don't remember him from our last adventure, he's the Somerville baseball coach.

Infamous for:

- NOT smiling,
- NEVER taking off his glasses
- Getting oddly gross stuff stuck in that crazy mustache of his, and
- Banning technology from all the land

This snowman resembled Rod so much, I wouldn't be surprised if it came to life and started yelling at us to run laps in the snow! Don't believe me?! Here's a side-by-side comparison. Go ahead, see for yourself.

Scary, isn't it?!

But poor Snow Rod, he was all alone - so we got to work and made him his own little snowy crew.

We did all this before Momma Mia's opened. Talk about a productive day, huh?

Meet the others in the snow family:

Billy Snowbuns

Holly Jolly

Mr. Bells

Bob

We stood back and admired the snowman village - we agreed, Bob was one of our favorites.

I was getting ready to build a snow cat when suddenly everyone started to sing. YES - SING!!! From behind her back, Harper pulled out a chocolate chip birthday cake and *Happy Birthday* was sung at the loudest level, EVER.

Don't tell me you forgot it was my birthday?!

I know this may sound crazy - but in that moment, it didn't matter if we ever figured out who Doc was, or what the reward may be. I got some of the best friends out there and that's all that matters!

But then it was time to blow out the candles and make a wish. Let's be real, finding the reward at the end of the scavenger hunt was my #1 birthday wish (even if I have the coolest friends EVER).

chomp chomp

HOLY MOLY that tasted really good.

But there was NO TIME to digest because...

WE DID IT AGAIN!

We got distracted by the delicious birthday cake and forgot about Clue #2. So, we ...

RAN
ALL
THE WAY TO
MOMMA MIA'S

We ran as fast as cheetahs chasing a Cheeto. We could barely get words out. We were huffing and puffing as we walked through the door.

we
Deep breath

need
another deep breath

to
get another deep breath

talk man, is this what happens when you turn one year older?!

Sunny stepped in and blurted out,

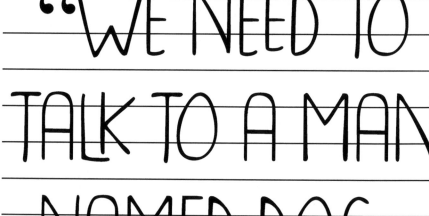

"WE NEED TO TALK TO A MAN NAMED DOC - NOW!"

The moment the words left Sunny's lips: a door creaked open. I could only see a big, old, worn boot at first.

No way, no way. Somebody pinch me.

Doc is... Doc is....

Hey Sunny- you know how I do things... It's all about leaving the customer wanting more! There's no better way to add suspense than to make people wait - so I'm passing the journal to you.

Talk about suspense, right?! Like who is Doc?! ...

Make me proud, Jack

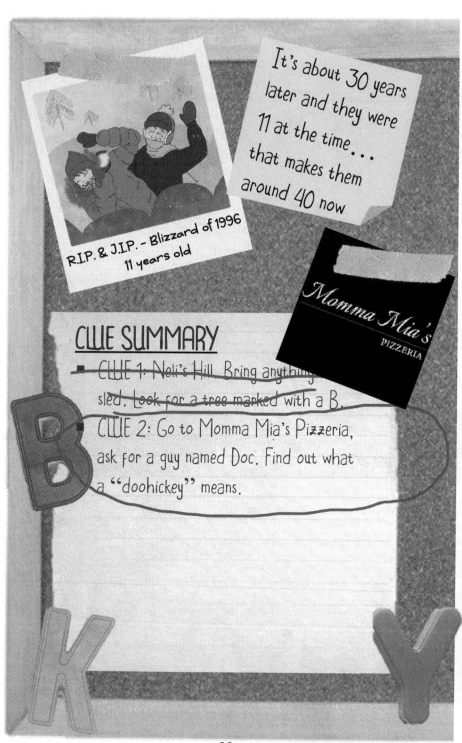

It's about 30 years later and they were 11 at the time... that makes them around 40 now

R.I.P. & J.I.P. - Blizzard of 1996
11 years old

Momma Mia's
PIZZERIA

CLUE SUMMARY

CLUE 1: Neli's Hill. Bring anything sled. Look for a tree marked with a B.

CLUE 2: Go to Momma Mia's Pizzeria, ask for a guy named Doc. Find out what a "doohickey" means.

What is a doohickey?

Written on time capsule:
R.I.P. + J.I.P '96

These kids must have lived on Bay Road and buried the capsule then

It's me again, Sunny!!

ENTRY SIX

Still Wednesday, January 5

Doohickey

Stuff about me

LOVES: Arts and crafts, playing basketball, and spaghetti

LOVES EVEN MORE: My cat George, the beach, VOLLEYBALL.

Doc is... Doc is... HUH? He's not so scary after all. In fact, he greeted us with the biggest smile. "What can I do for you kids?" He wouldn't believe us if we told him, so we *showed him.*

Time Capsule Clue #2
You made it this far, oh what a thrill;
How much fun - sledding down Neli's Hill.

This next clue is a bit more tricky,
But someone will help you figure out this doohickey.

Make your way to the best pizza place in town,
Ask for Doc and remember to
'smile, never frown'.

Our eyes stayed glued to Doc as he read the clue. It first seemed like he was in shock, but he soon began to smile. "Wait here kiddos. I'll be right back."

Doc returned with eyes glowing of excitement and wonder. He said, "It's been 30 years since...

... since the Blizzard of '96. Best year of my life. Besides the day my kids were born. ❄

... since a little bitty Rita walked through that same pizza shop door and had me hold on to a secret clue for her.

With one hearty laugh, he hugged us all
and handed over
an envelope.

"30 years, but I
finally get to
see what is in
this envelope.
I haven't
peeked, not
once."

DO NOT OPEN UNLESS YOU
HAVE CLUE #2

DOOHICKEY
inside

I emptied the envelope
to find another torn paper with a
clue and a black rectangular device (that MUST be the
doohickey!)

Doc said, "What do we have here? A camera from back in the day. Taking pictures was my favorite thing to do. Getting them developed with friends was my kind of Friday night fun. But enough of the flashbacks - let's see what Rita had to say."

Time Capsule Clue #3

You found a device that captures time,
Go to the corner store - camera photo line.

Take the last few pictures as you trek along the way,
They used to be 10 cents a print, not sure what you'll pay.

The next clue will be hidden in the pictures you'll see,
It'll lead you to the place where you once learned,
"one, two, three."

"I don't even know how to work a camera like this..."
– Duke

"The clue says something is hidden in the pictures – that means they took some pictures on the camera." – Kolten

"How the heck do we see pictures on the camera?! There is no screen."
– Harper

"This is awesome! We have about ten pictures left to take!!"
– Sunny

"Where did we learn one, two, three?"
– Jayden

Convos about the capsule clue

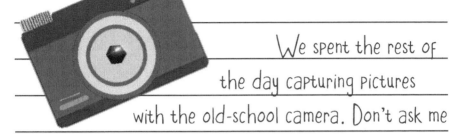 We spent the rest of the day capturing pictures with the old-school camera. Don't ask me where the picture went once we snapped them. They somehow stayed inside the camera. Can you believe that?

Then, we took the camera to the store, just like the clue said, and waited for the pictures to be "developed." *Side note: We learned that this meant printing the pictures out!*

This *doohickey* was filled with surprises, it STILL WORKED after 30 YEARS!! Sixty minutes later, we were looking at a mixture of pictures - some were taken by us and others by the time capsule kids.

Check it out!! Below are some of the pictures WE took... On the next page are the *old* pictures taken by the capsule kids, RIP and JIP.

Our pictures

Wait!! Does that look like the tire swing at the old, abandoned house? Why would RIP and JIP take a picture of this spot?!

I have so many questions, there are so many clues. Camera clues, Capsule clues, Rhyming Riddles. Where do we go from here?!

Signing out - tired and confused, Sunny

It's about 30 years later and they were 11 at the time... that makes them around 40 now

R.I.P. & J.I.P. - Blizzard of 1996
11 years old

Momma Mia's PIZZERIA

CLUE SUMMARY

- CLUE 1: Neli's Hill. Bring anything but sled. Look for a tree marked with a B.
- CLUE 2: Go to Momma Mia's Pizzeria, ask for a guy named Doc. Find out what a "doohickey" means.
- CLUE 3: Take pictures, develop. Go to the place where you learned 1, 2, 3

What is a doohickey?

IT'S A CAMERA!!

Written on time capsule:
R.I.P. + J.I.P '96

These kids must have lived on Bay Road and buried the capsule then

Pictures taken by R.I.P. + J.I.P.

1. A picture of some old, dusty room. With cobwebs, EVERYWHERE

2. The tire swing at the abandoned house

3. Somerville Charter School

ENTRY SEVEN

Thursday, January 6
Oh, what a nightmare!

Me: Jayden Bell
Birthday: January 1

About me:

- Sneaker lover
- Basketball obsessed
- Can always be found riding my bike around the neighborhood
- Ellie follows me EVERYWHERE

ATTENTION READERS:

We interrupt this
SCAVENGER HUNT
for a
SOMERVILLE SNOW BOWL!!

I know what you're thinking. We have NO time to waste and we need to finish the scavenger hunt. BUT we were feeling stumped, puzzled, confused.

We didn't know where the clues were leading us. It was clear we needed a break! A little distraction would do us good. Somerville Snowbowl - here we come!!

We recruited ALL the Somerville kids and headed to the football field (Ace, Parker, Quinn, and Spence joined us). When we got to our field, we were SHOCKED to see our rivals, the Philly Blazers ON OUR FIELD. We wouldn't stand for this!

Side note: If you don't know who the Philly Blazers are, they are the cheaters from our baseball season!

SOMERVILLE BULLDOGS
VS
PHILLY BLAZERS
SNOWBOWL

Thursday, January 6

Winner earns title "Snow Bowl Champions."

Turn the page to activate awesome football sequence.

1st Quarter

The football field was COVERED in blankets and hills of snow. When someone was tackled it felt like hitting the fluffiest of fluffy pillows. Tackles were happening left and right; it was tied 7-7.

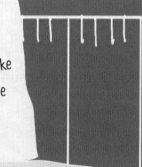

2nd Quarter

Parker "The Fridge" Reeves scored the second touchdown of the game. When he ran through the snow it was like a bulldozer paving the way. He cleared anything in his path, INCLUDING FOUR FEET OF SNOW.

3rd Quarter

We were down, 24-21. The streetlights were about to come on, which meant we were down to our last play. We would have one more try in the fourth quarter. It was all or nothing.

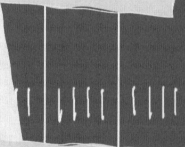

4th Quarter

Spence, a kid known for his smarts, thought of a plan. It was going to be risky and take a little grit. Exactly the stuff us Somerville kids are made of. He called it the

"Somerville Special."

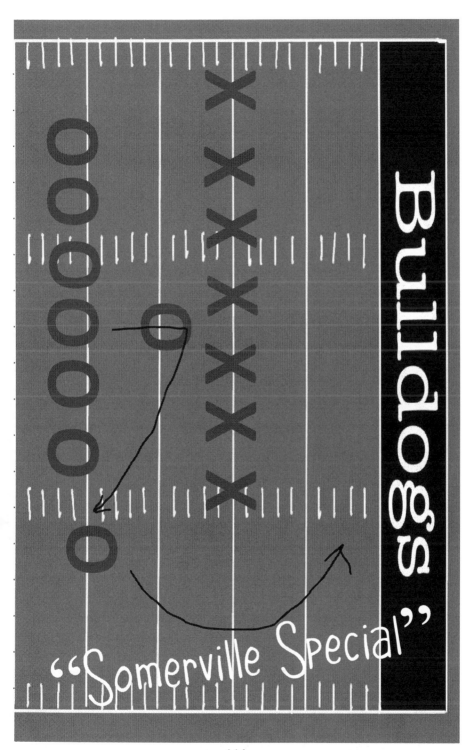

TOUCCHHHHHH DOWNNN!!!

Spence with the winning touchdown!

Bulldogs win, 27-24.

Somerville BULLDOGS Snow Bowl CHAMPS

We celebrated, we cheered, and we raised Spence on our shoulders. The school bell echoed our celebration, **ringing** in the distance.

Maybe tomorrow we would have a better idea how to handle this time capsule mystery. We were

SNOW BOWL CHAMPS

after all...

we could do anything!!

After football, me and Ellie headed home to defrost with a bowl of chicken noodle soup! I was so tired I fell asleep at the kitchen table, SITTING UP! Before I knew it, I heard Ellie yelling, "Jayden, Jayden why are you screaming?? WAKE UP! You're having a nightmare!"

It was too scary not to share, so I filled her in.

MY NIGHTMARE:

1   The school bell ringing (the one that sounds to start the day at school). WORST SOUND EVER.

2   But it was ringing OVER and OVER and OVER. It would NOT stop!

3   Principal Pringlensap stood at the entrance to the school, capturing us!!

Now repeat steps 1-3 over and over again. That was my nightmare.

WAIT—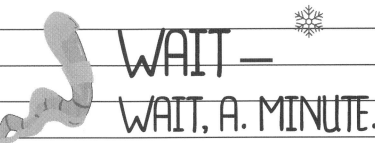
WAIT, A. MINUTE.

I started to jump up and down, I even kissed Ellie on the head (she screeched immediately and made a face that looked like she ate a mouthful of worms covered in mustard).

I figured it out, the next part of the clue. It wasn't a nightmare - it was a **SIGN**! Remember the clue said we need to go where we learned "one, two, three" and then there is the picture of the school they took....

It's the school!

We need to head to Somerville Charter!

This was important, I needed to tell the crew.

The plan for CLUE#3:

- WE ARE HEADED BACK TO SCHOOL
- Meet at the street corner tomorrow (when it starts to get dark out, but not dark enough to bring on the streetlights)
- Pack bags and our flashlights - who knows what kind of trouble we are going to run into

expect the unexpected and prepare, my POP-POP always says!!

Me, I am writing in the journal now, instead of packing.
I don't know what's going to happen to us
tomorrow... Really, stop and think about it... We are
headed to school (when it's closed), IN THE DARK.

NO
- parents
- kids
- teachers

Well, technically, if you believe the rumors, Pringlesnap
WILL be there. Don't remember? Rumor
is rotten old Pringlesnap lives
at school,
in a dungeon.

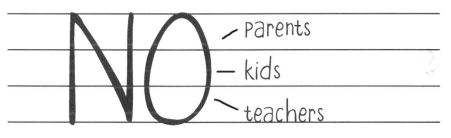

ALL YEAR LONG.
Guess we're going to find out...

One thing is crystal clear - the odds are definitely stacked against us! Sooooo it's important to end my entry and bring the journal on this mission. If we do make it out UNHARMED, I'll pass it to the next kid.

Signing out & petrified,
    Jayden and Ellie

Again, Jayden?!
When are you going to RENEMBER to leaf me space in theze journals?! There is always time for little sister takeoverz.

I have importaner thingz to say. Check out my game I played with my friend.

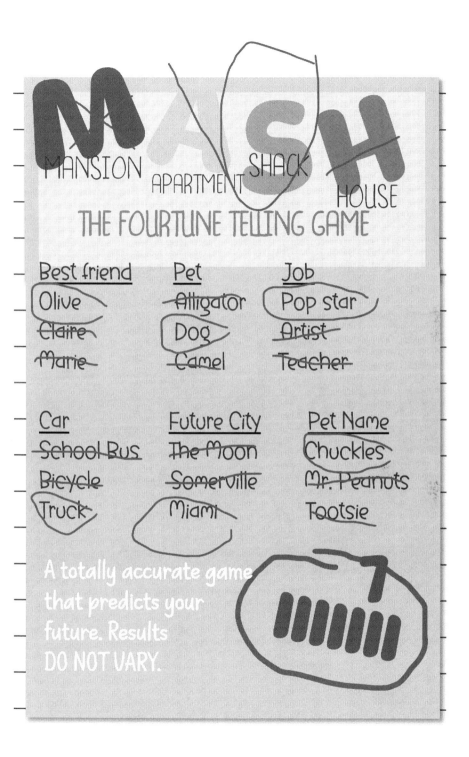

MASH

MANSION APARTMENT SHACK HOUSE

THE FOURTUNE TELLING GAME

Best friend
Olive
Claire
Marie

Pet
Alligator
Dog
Camel

Job
Pop star
Artist
Teacher

Car
School Bus
Bicycle
Truck

Future City
The Moon
Somerville
Miami

Pet Name
Chuckles
Mr. Peanuts
Tootsie

A totally accurate game that predicts your future. Results DO NOT VARY.

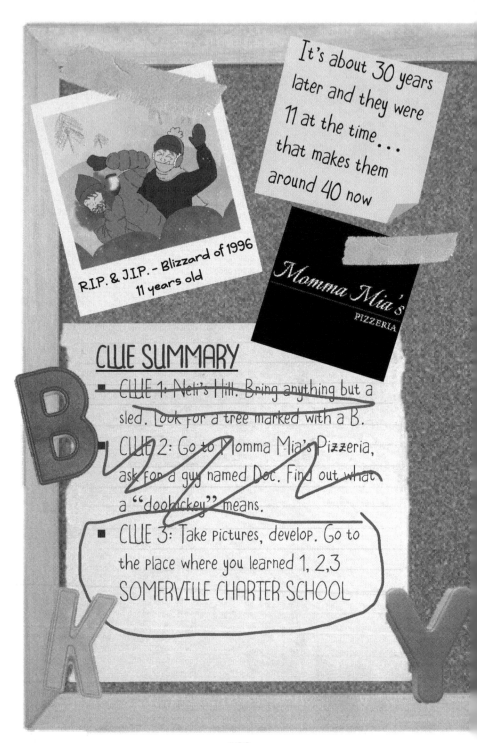

It's about 30 years later and they were 11 at the time... that makes them around 40 now

R.I.P. & J.I.P. - Blizzard of 1996
11 years old

Momma Mia's
PIZZERIA

CLUE SUMMARY

- CLUE 1: Neli's Hill. Bring anything but a sled. Look for a tree marked with a B.
- CLUE 2: Go to Momma Mia's Pizzeria, ask for a guy named Doc. Find out what a "doohickey" means.
- CLUE 3: Take pictures, develop. Go to the place where you learned 1, 2, 3 SOMERVILLE CHARTER SCHOOL

What is a doohickey?

IT'S A CAMERA!!

CLUE #3: Picture of the school on the camera makes sense now! We need to head to school!

Written on time capsule:
R.I.P. + J.I.P '96

These kids must have lived on Bay Road and buried the capsule then

by R.I.P. + J.I.P.

1. A picture of some old, dusty room. With cobwebs, EVERYWHERE
2. The tire swing at the abandoned house
3. Somerville Charter School

ENTRY EIGHT

Friday, January 8
Back to school

KOLT 'THE BOLT'
is back!!

Sorry but absolutely NO time for cute, little things about me! You know I love baseball.

I NEED TO PICK UP WHERE JAYDEN LEFT OFF.

Don't assume anything. Just because Jayden passed the journal to me doesn't mean we were not harmed. Here's how it all went down.

We met at the corner and headed to school. First, we had to pass the abandoned house. To do so, rules HAD to be followed.

☑ Rule #1 - no talking,

☑ Rule #2 - no looking,

☑ Rule #3 - no breathing...

When we finally arrived at school, we were STARTLED by the school bells ringing, NON-STOP. Weird. No one was supposed to be here, why were they sounding?

I heard Ellie whisper to Jayden, "It's just like your nightmare!" INSERT chills, goosebumps, shivers. I was officially spooked.

A third bell alarmed, slowly a side door creaked open. I peeked inside and yelled "hello." My voice echoed throughout the entire school. It was lifeless - and COMPLETELY dark. We pulled out our flashlights and slowly entered. Each step vibrated the lockers... and it smelled, weird, like rotten pencil shavings and dirty gym shorts.

If it wasn't for this time capsule clue, I would turn my behind back around and head straight for home. Actually, I'd **RUN** - like sprint really, really fast.

This is what scary movies are made of. You'll see what I mean.

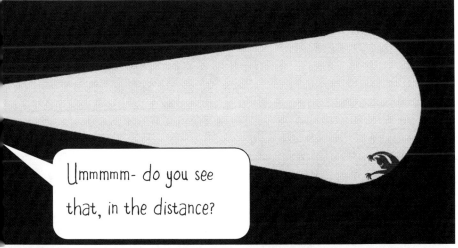

128

IT'S PRINGLESNAP!!!
OMG- RUNNNNNN
Don't eat us, PLEASE!
The rumors are TRUE! She really does live here!!
DUKE- THAT SMELLS!

We found ourselves face-to-face with Principal Pringlesnap. Luckily, Sunny didn't miss a beat. Without hesitation she pleaded . . .

"Pllleasseeeee let us finish what we started. We NEED to find the final clue. We NEED to know who RIP and JIP are. We just NEED to figure it all out. Once and for all! The clues, the treasure, the people!"

Principal Pringlesnap stared at us. I tried to avoid eye contact. She remained silent. So silent I could practically hear the crickets roaming the hallway. Until finally . . .

"Here is what you'll have to do,
See that door? Walk on through.

Clean and clean and clean some more.
I want it to look like it did before.

Back in the day, the floors shined bright.
Oh, it was such a beautiful sight!"

Poof, she was gone.

Duke turned to us, "It's all ruined. Everything. The time capsule, the fun, our snowy adventure. We'll be here cleaning this old place until the cows come home."

"Dude, who cares about cleaning... How did she just disappear like that??? Freaky."

Sunny shouted, "You both need to relax! Pringelsnap told us to clean this room, so let's just clean the room and move on. Forget this snowy adventure ever happened."

We walked through the door - it was the Somerville Hall of Fame.

This room was stacked with bookcases of trophies, boxes, and cobwebs... SO. MANY. COBWEBS.
Then I realized it - we had seen this room before! But where?!?!

In typical Sunny form, she handed us a to-do list...
Hopefully, when we finish, we can solve this mystery.

Old Smelly Room To-Do List

Kolt - alphabetize books

Duke - Try not to fart *again*

Jack - Closet organization, hang jerseys

Ellie & Jayden - cobweb duty

Harper - Pringlesnap lookout

Bash Bros - dust, sweep, mop, play some music on the radio I know you stuffed in your backpacks

Jack found a stack of books in a closet, "Hey Kolt, HUGE stack of books coming your way." He launched them through the air. Seriously?? He could have walked them over.

Interestingly, they all landed in a pile, except ONE. This one ripped in half. Split down the spine with a page ripped to the side. "Poor book." Harper walked over and sat beside it, reading the torn page.

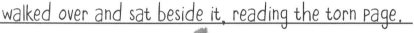

"Looks like an old yearbook page. Look at some of these hair styles . . .

"UMMMMMMMM, wait. Stop talking. Does anyone see what I see? Look real close . . ."

Rita Ingrid Pringlesnap
The final clue is back where you started,
Go to the tire swing and find where the heart is

Charles Henry Rodriguez
There's no I in team, but there is ME.
And I am THE BEST!

That picture says

PRINGLESNAP.

Her initials spell

R.I.P.

There is only one

Pringlesnap to roam

this Earth...

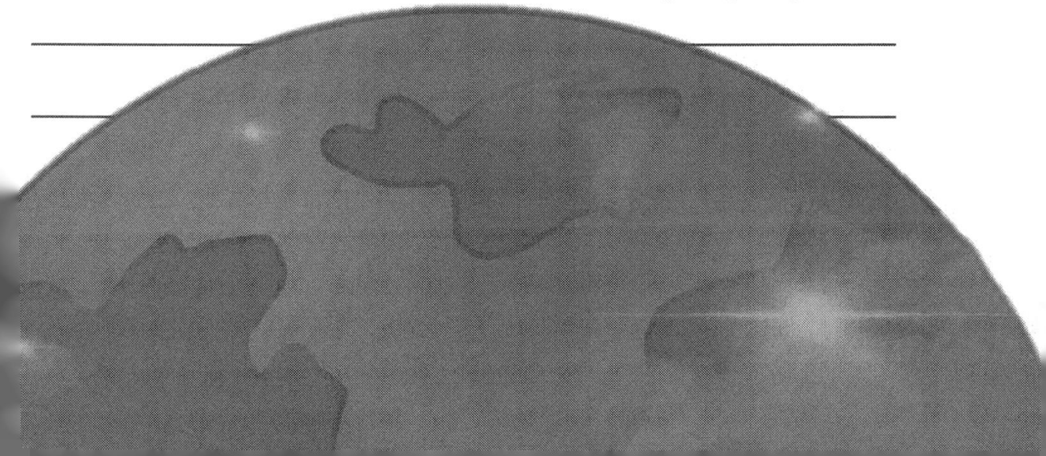

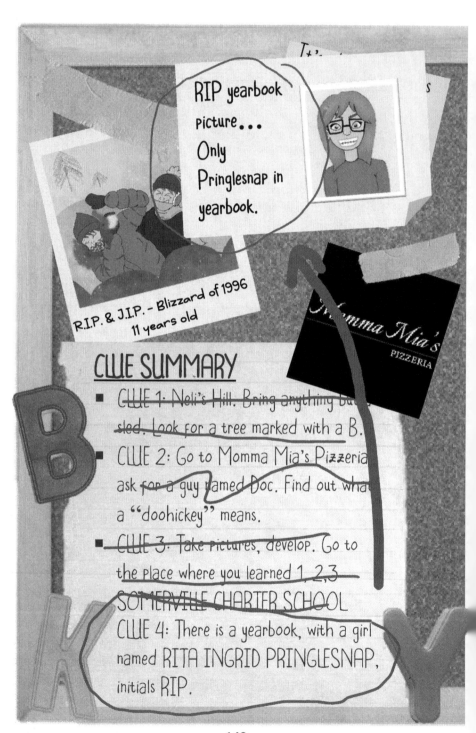

RIP yearbook picture... Only Pringlesnap in yearbook.

R.I.P. & J.I.P. – Blizzard of 1996
11 years old

Momma Mia's PIZZERIA

CLUE SUMMARY

- ~~CLUE 1: Neli's Hill. Bring anything but a sled.~~ Look for a tree marked with a B.
- CLUE 2: Go to Momma Mia's Pizzeria ask for a guy named Doc. Find out what a "doohickey" means.
- ~~CLUE 3: Take pictures, develop.~~ Go to the place where you learned 1, 2, 3 ~~SOMERVILLE CHARTER SCHOOL~~
  CLUE 4: There is a yearbook, with a girl named RITA INGRID PRINGLESNAP, initials RIP.

What is a doohickey?

Written on time capsule:
R.I.P. + J.I.P '96

These kids must have lived on Bay Road and apsule then

CLUE #3: Picture of the school on the camera makes sense now! We need to head to school!

by R.I. . .I.P.

1. A picture of some old, dusty room. With cobwebs, EVERYWHERE
2. The tire swing at the abandoned house
3. Somerville Charter School

ENTRY NINE

Still Friday, January 8

PRINGLESNAP

DUKE,
back at it

Keep on reading, the surprises don't stop!!!

Silent.

Quiet.

Stunned.

This cannot be who we think it is. It CANNOT BE. It had to be some kind of mistake or misunderstanding, right?

We recapped our journey, what got us here... there were some things we never noticed before.

There is only one kid in the whole entire yearbook with the initials RIP, and the last name ends in... PRINGLESNAP.

Pringlesnap was talking in rhyme when she sent us to the storage room. Who randomly talks in rhyme?!

Remember, the guy we met at Momma Mia's, Doc? He referenced a girl named, "Rita" (at the time we didn't know it was in reference to *the* Rita Pringlesnap. (Do teachers and principals even have first names?)

It all somehow started to make sense. But we still couldn't wrap our heads around it. The person responsible for the most epic scavenger hunt of all times may actually be... No, no, no. It just can NOT be

Principal Pringlesnap.

The one who NEVER cancels school, and lives in a dungeon, the one who enjoys 102 question math tests, the one who has claws for toes!!

We must have said her name too many times because

POOF...

There she was, standing before us. How on Earth does she keep doing that?!?

"30 years. 30 *long* years to figure it out.

30 years since I planted that time capsule...

And let me tell you something, kids...

... I miss the good old days of running home to Bay Road with my friends, finishing my homework AT LIGHTNING SPEED and playing outside until the streetlights came on...

... I miss laughing so hard that my belly ached and my eyes teared...

... I miss summer days spent at Boyle Pond and summer nights riding bikes to Momma Mia's...

... I miss the kids I grew up with on Bay Road (What. A. Crew.) But mostly, I miss Jenny, the one in the picture who helped me with the time capsule...

... When we got older, we went our separate ways. That's what happens when you grow up, I guess. But when I moved away from Bay Road, well, I left a piece of my heart there too...

... It's been 30 years. Wow! Where does the time go? When you mentioned a time capsule adventure, I just knew it was mine... it was like rewinding time, time to a place when my heart was complete."

A suddenly transformed Pringlesnap became stuck, totally frozen. I am talking about ice cube kind of frozen. We snapped our fingers, clapped our hands.

"Helllllooooo - Principal Pringlesnap. Can you hear us?" She didn't respond. We were going to be in even bigger trouble. We froze her, messed up this entire scavenger hunt...

WE ARE NEVER GOING TO FIGURE THIS THING OUT!

Why is she frozen? Please say something! Please!!!!
Why is she frozen? Please say something! Please!!!!
Why is she frozen? Please say something! Please!!!!
Why is she frozen? Please say something! Please!!!!
Why is she frozen? Please say something! Please!!!!
Why is she frozen? Please say something! Please!!!!
Why is she frozen? Please say something! Please!!!!
Why is she frozen? Please say something! Please!!!!
Why is she frozen? Please say something! Please!!!!
Why is she frozen? Please say something! Please!!!!
Why is she frozen? Please say something! Please!!!!
Why is she frozen? Please say something! Please!!!!
Why is she frozen? Please say something! Please!!!!
Why is she frozen? Please say something! Please!!!!
Why is she frozen? Please say something! Please!!!!
Why is she frozen? Please say something! Please!!!!

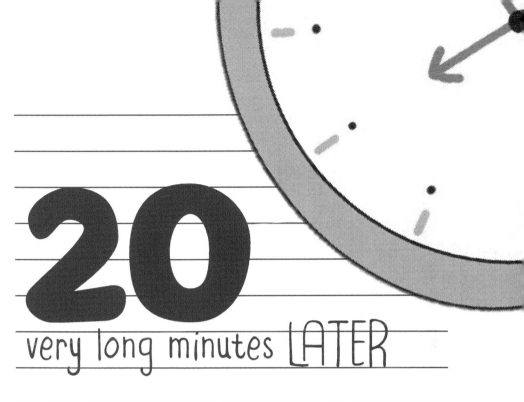

20
very long minutes LATER

Why is she frozen? Please say something! Please!!!!

Why is she frozen? Please say something! Please!!!!

Ok... let's think about this... "Hey Jack, one of the last things she said before she went all ICE CUBE-LIKE was something about rewinding time... something with time and her heart?! What do you think that means?"

Suddenly, she spoke! GREAT NEWS - WE DIDN'T BREAK HER!

"Sunny - tell me where the next clue has taken you..."

"We have no idea... we figured out you were the kid behind the time capsule, but we don't know who JIP is and we have no idea where to go next. All we have left is that old yearbook page."

"That's it, that's it!!!! Sunny, look *under* my yearbook picture, what is written?!"

Rita Ingrid Pringlesnap
The final clue is back where you started,
Go to the tire swing and find where the heart is

Look at that, it says:
The final clue is back where you started,
Go to the tire swing and find where the
heart is.

We all stared at each other...
Principal Pringlesnap connected us
to the final clue. We knew
exactly what to do. The clue
said, 'back where you started'.
Duh, that was easy! We had to
head over to Bay Road, where
the capsule adventures began.

It was part two of this clue that made us uneasy. We knew of a tire swing on Bay Road, but it's on *haunted* grounds, behind a *haunted,* abandoned house. Rumor has it no one has lived there in centuries. Dude, wait, that's a lie. *Haunted* ghosts and goblins live there. But you see where I'm going with this, right?!

We CANNOT go there!

If you don't remember, let me remind you:

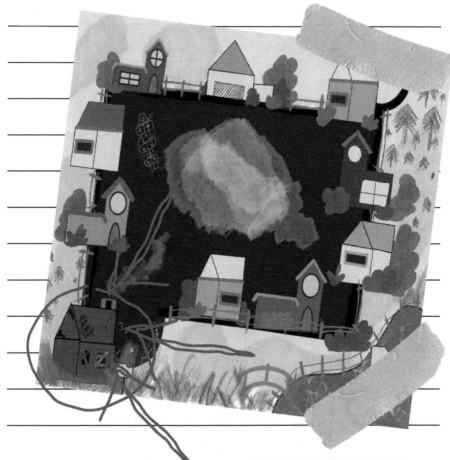

There. The abandoned house!

Should we go there?

I didn't like the sound of this. But we've come this far. I wasn't going to let some old scary house hold us back. We needed to finish this adventure. With or without the crew, I WAS GOING.

I'm in.

Me too.

Let's go!

Well, it was settled. We would go back to Bay Road, get to that tire swing, and finish this time capsule mission. There was only one thing we had to do before we made our way back...

"Principal Pringlesnap, do you want to come with us?"

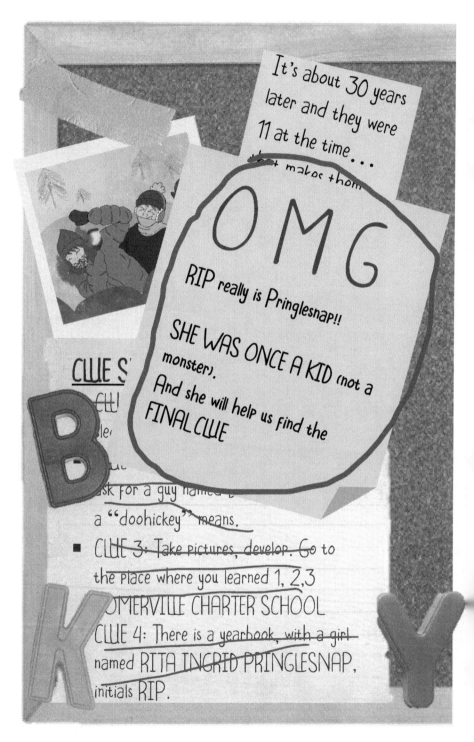

BEWARE:
You are about to cross
enemy lines . . .

ENTRY TEN

Still Friday, January 8
To the abandoned house we go

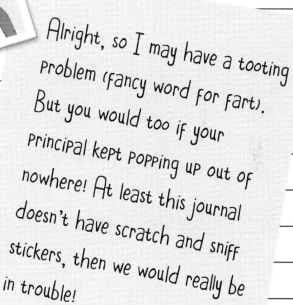

Still me,
~~Duke!~~

Alright, so I may have a tooting problem (fancy word for fart). But you would too if your principal kept popping up out of nowhere! At least this journal doesn't have scratch and sniff stickers, then we would really be in trouble!

Before we knew it, we were at the abandoned house, watching the tire swing sway in the breeze.

I thought it would feel weird with Principal Pringlesnap here with us. BUT it didn't. She was once a Bay Road kid, she lived in Somerville, she fits right in.

No one has been so daring to step foot on the sidewalk in front of this house - never even stepped foot on the grass. The fact that we were making our way towards the backyard was confusing and scary, yet gave me a thrill.

I guess this is why Sunny calls me a dare devil.

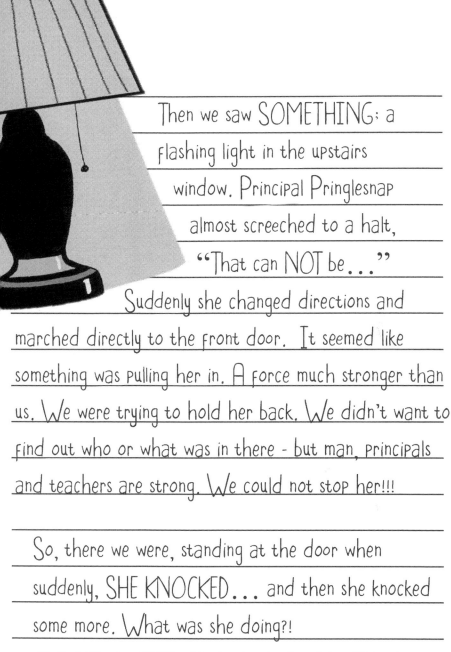

Then we saw SOMETHING: a flashing light in the upstairs window. Principal Pringlesnap almost screeched to a halt, "That can NOT be..." Suddenly she changed directions and marched directly to the front door. It seemed like something was pulling her in. A force much stronger than us. We were trying to hold her back. We didn't want to find out who or what was in there - but man, principals and teachers are strong. We could not stop her!!!

So, there we were, standing at the door when suddenly, SHE KNOCKED... and then she knocked some more. What was she doing?!

SHE KEPT KNOCKING

I wanted to run the other way.
I wanted to scream for my blankie
(don't tell anyone about that).
There's a flashing light.
In a house that has been empty for
decades.
WHAT WAS SHE THINKING?!

We stood still waiting to meet the mysterious person (or demon) behind the door and I noticed Pringlesnap's hand shaking... Was she nervous? Does she actually have feelings? If Principal Pringlesnap is missing a piece of her heart, I guess that makes her -

My thoughts were interrupted by the door creaking open. Slowly, a HUGE figure emerged, and it started to say something.

Well, it MUMBLED something.

Mailbox by the front door...

SUDDENLY, it was peeling its skin off.

Ok, maybe not skin. It peeled layers off. Leaving mounds of coats, scarves, hats, and blankets on the doorstep (Sheesh - I guess there's no heat in the house?!) What was left under those layers? Well, it was a woman.

"Jenny????"

Pringlesnap replied.

Then, we weren't looking at our school principal anymore. But two long lost friends reunited!!! They did the coolest secret handshake I have ever seen and both said,

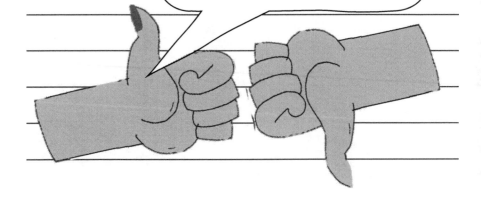

"No matter the distance,
near or far,
RIP and JIP will always be
in the back yardy-yar-yar."

Like little kids, they bolted to the backyard of the old ~~abandoned~~ house and Jenny hopped on the tire swing. Pringlesnap pushed her, sending her soaring in the air - over and over again. We ran after them. It looked like so much fun!!!

Do you want to join? Turn the page!!

"Well kids, here it is!! What do you think?"

We stared at the tree.
Maybe all this fresh air
and fun got to their
heads, I mean it's a nice
tree and all, but sheesh.
Boyle Woods has 10,000
just like this one.

"Ummm, it's a real nice
tire swing you got there...
can we try it?" They didn't
answer, Jenny and
Principal Pringlesnap
started to dig, FAST, at
the base of the tree.

Weirdest. Day. Ever.

They didn't even look up at us. They

just

kept

digging.

There was one thing to do...

WE
JOINED
IN

We dug and dug and dug some more. Man, what do they call this, déjà vu? Isn't it? When it feels like you are reliving the same moment? This was EXACTLY how our adventure began, with me and Sunny DIGGING.

We didn't notice when they stopped, but Pringlesnap and Jenny stood arm in arm with smiles stretched from ear to ear. We KEPT ON DIGGING UNTIL we heard a loud

KLANK

Oh BOY! I think we're close. This is seriously the same sound we heard when we found the time capsule! We pulled a HUGE BOX from the ground, and ripped it open to find...

FINAL TIME CAPSULE CLUE:

You're so close to solving the time capsule mystery,
Gather clue pieces, the rest will be history.
What happens is magical, your eyes won't deceive,
BUT it'll only happen if you BELIEVE.
Once all the clues become one,
Flip it over and read for more time capsule fun.
The message revealed is special, you'll see,
It's one you'll remember FOR-EV-ER, this we guarantee.

Holy macaroni, holy Duke of

Casserole, holy cow, holy...

Good thing we brought Pringlesnap along. She shouted,
"Chop, chop, hurry up everyone! Gather all the
clues. Hurry, bring them over here!"

We pulled clues from our pockets and laid them on the grass. Harper arranged them in number order.

Suddenly, the ground *vibrated* beneath our feet.

It felt like an earthquake. Well, I never actually felt an earthquake before. BUT I'd imagine THIS is what it would feel like. Even the tree shook HARD in the wind. Hold on, WIND? Where did that sudden gust come from? As if it had a mind of its' own, the time capsule clues started to mimic the tree, rattling back and forth. THEN, they became ONE - just like the clue said! Almost like there was a force pulling them together.

It was electric!!

For real - the clues started to GLOW when they came together. This had to be magic, right?

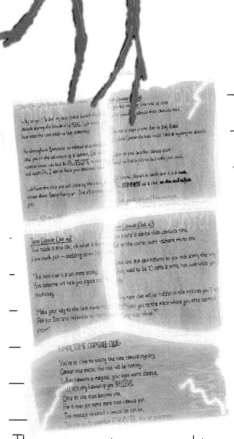

There was only one possible other reason to describe what was happening. I was still asleep, and this was all a dream. "Quick, someone do something!" Leave it to the Bash Bros. They poured a bucket of water, OVER. MY. HEAD... AND I WAS SOAKED. Meaning it was totally not a dream, this was real life AND I was still staring at that glowing piece of paper.

Even more impossible but **ABSOLUTELY** true...
LOOK at what started

falling

from

the

tree.

1989

183

It felt like Christmas morning! Sunny started talking while holding back tears, "Guys, these aren't just random gifts from some random gift-giving tree. These are the rewards we wished for back when this wild and crazy time capsule adventure began."

Ode to a Backyard Kid (BYK)

You cracked the code, it's the end;
One final word, go grab your friends.
Remember you have only one childhood,
Fill it with memories, make it good.
Meet at the playground, front yard, or alleyway,
Fill your days with nothing but laughter and play.
Go swimming, ride bikes, trade baseball cards,
Play tackle football in the front yard.
Create secret handshakes, bracelets, or dances;
Be daring, go ahead and take some chances.
No matter how much you'll want to delay,
You *will* get older, revisiting the past in replay.
And no matter how old you really may get,
It's your childhood memories you won't forget.
Store such memories in a jar with a lid,
Recall them often and you'll forever be a *backyard kid*.

-Rita Ingrid Pringesnap and Jenny Isabelle Porter, BFF
The *Original* Backyard Kids, 1996

CLICK!!!!! Have you ever tried really, really, really hard to figure something out and then ALL OF A SUDDEN, it just CLICKS. Literally, that just happened. It all makes sense now. FINALLY. I get it...the whole point of this time capsule experience.

And I FINALLY understand the magnetic letters in the capsule and what BYK stands for... BYK

Do you get it, too? Did you hear the CLICK? If not, let me explain...

I looked at the people standing in front of me...
Sunny, Jack, Kolt, the Bash Bros, Jayden, Ellie,
Harper. I thought of Somerville.

I always knew I was lucky to live on THE BEST street
in Somerville. But now I've learned that it's not about
the actual street or the city. It's about them - the
people in our lives and the moments we share.

I can't help but smile as I think about this adventure.
This was one of the best weeks of my life - it doesn't
get much better than a magical tree, right? **Wrong.** I
have my friends, my memories, and the fun times we'll
share in the future. Even when we get super old and
wrinkly, like in our 40's, we'll still be connected. I now
know why it's possible. It's because we are all...

backyard kids

RIP & JIP '23
Backyard Kids Forever

BFF

I still can't believe we learned this from our principal and her childhood BFF!

ENTRY ELEVEN

Monday, January 11
Back to school, FOR REAL

Still your boy,
Duke here!

Three days later...

All the snow has melted...

Goodbye Snow Bob, Snow Rod and friends...

Time to head back to school...

I entered 1st period math class dreading the 102 - question test. Found my seat, unpacked my lunch, and looked to the chalkboard to see what our daily agenda was going to be.

"What the heck? No math test? What's going on here... ?"

"Good morning Somerville Charter School and welcome back! Principal Pringlesnap here... Today for lunch we have sloppy joes with broccoli. Next, please notice the school math test has been canceled. That is my little gift to you all. You are welcome.
Now, look under your desks. You will find directions to your *newest* assignment, my second gift to you all."

The room filled with kids moaning and groaning...
Come on, swapping one assignment for another? Is she
really the same diabolical principal? I thought she
changed!!!

We looked under our desks and continued to listen.

Principal Pringlesnap continued, "Oh, I would like you
to call me Mrs. Pringlesnap. Yes, Mrs. Pringlesnap it is
from here on out, please!"

Principal Pringlesnap. I mean,
Mrs. Pringlensap read the
assignment over the
loudspeaker...

Somerville Charter School
Time Capsule Assignment

Now that I have your full attention,
There are some things I need to mention.
Boys and girls, welcome back to school!
The blizzard kept us home - wasn't that cool?
I shockingly had an amazing time,
and was reminded of memories, totally sublime!
I am here to tell you about a school-wide project,
First things first, collect an object.
Something special that tells a story,
Or something you're proud of and portrays your glory.
Gather 5 items and write about each one,
Then place them in the capsule until you're done.
Grab a shovel and dig a deep, big hole.
Bury the time capsule - that's the goal!
Once you complete this, your challenge is done.
Then go head outside and make sure to have some

Backyard Kid
FUN!

There was no question what items would be in my time capsule. I hope a group of kids just like us finds it in 30 years. When they do, they'll have no clue what kind of adventure they're in for... but I guarantee it will end by a magical tree that sits behind a *not so abandoned house.*

Somerville Time Capsule Map
by BYK '23

N W E S

Somerville BULLDOGS Snow Bowl CHAMPS

R.I.P. & J.I.P. - Blizzard of 1ˢ
11 years old

Blizzard of 2023
Bay Road

Dear kid reading this book,

You opened our top-secret journal and finished it! That means you are officially part of the Backyard Family! Do you want to know what it's like to make your own time capsule? Follow the assignment from Principal Pringlesnap (oops, we mean MRS. Pringlesnap, on page 198).

Once you complete the time capsule challenge, let "The Backyard Kids" know by sending us an email, finding us on social media, or hollering as you pass us on the streets of Philadelphia!

From,
The Backyard Kids

BYK book club

Find The Snowflakes: Math Extension

The Backyard Kids hid snowflakes throughout the story.

- How many snowflakes can you find on page 15?
- How many snowflakes, in all, can you find in the entire book?
- How many more snowflakes are on page 15 than page 84?

Words To Explore: Turn and Talk

Find these words in the story. What does the word mean? Turn and Talk. If needed, look up the definition of the word in the dictionary!

Commence	Hoax	Interrupted	Underestimate
Productive	Petrified	Distracted	Developed

Chat About The Book: Comprehension & Extension

- Entry 1: Why does Duke join in Operation Snow Dance? Do you have a superstition to help make snow fall from the sky?
- Entry 4: The kids create a Reward Wishlist. Imagine you were part of the Bay Road crew. What would be on your Reward Wishlist? Why?
- Entry 6: Foreshadowing is a time when the writer gives a hint about what is to come. On page 103, we see 3 pictures from the time capsule kids. What are these pictures foreshadowing?
- Entry 9: On pages 143 through 148, Principal Pringlesnap transforms her look. Why do you think she is making this transformation?
- Entry 10: Who is Jenny? Why is she important to Principal Pringlesnap?
- Entry 11: What did Principal Pringlesnap cancel? What is the new assignment? Why do you think Principal Pringlesnap wants the kids to call her Mrs. Pringlesnap now?

About the Authors

Regina Oakes and Danielle Devine hit # 1 in the 'Outdoors & Sports' category on Amazon with the new release of their first book, 'The Backyard Kids - Baseball Edition'.

Now, they are back with the second book in The Backyard Kid series! Their books in this series capture the life of ordinary kids experiencing not so ordinary events. Giving children a voice, their books are told from the perspective of children as they pass a journal from one friend to the next.

Regina, a special education teacher and Danielle, a university professor and registered nurse, met as neighbors in 2013. Little did they know at that time, aligned lifelong dreams and passion for teaching would lead to their collaboration of writing children's books. When not writing, Regina and Danielle are moms, educators, neighbors, and friends. They enjoy Philadelphia sports, spending time with family, and being full-blown sport moms.

Read more

WORRY LESS
be a backyard kid!

Follow us:

Be the first to know about new releases, giveaways, and special promotions. Ask your parent or guardian to follow us on socials.

 The Backyard Kids

 the_backyard_kids_215

 thebackyardkids215

Contact us:

We really want to hear from you! We TRULY mean it! Shoot us an email at backyardkids215@gmail.com
Send us pictures, drawings, or write us a note to say hi!!

Want more:

You can purchase ALL our books on Amazon. We have blank journals, coloring books, and activity books! We also have BYK Merch. Thank you for supporting The Backyard Kids!

 Use this QR code to buy 'The Backyard Kids - Baseball Edition' now!

Made in the USA
Middletown, DE
06 January 2024

47332500R00120